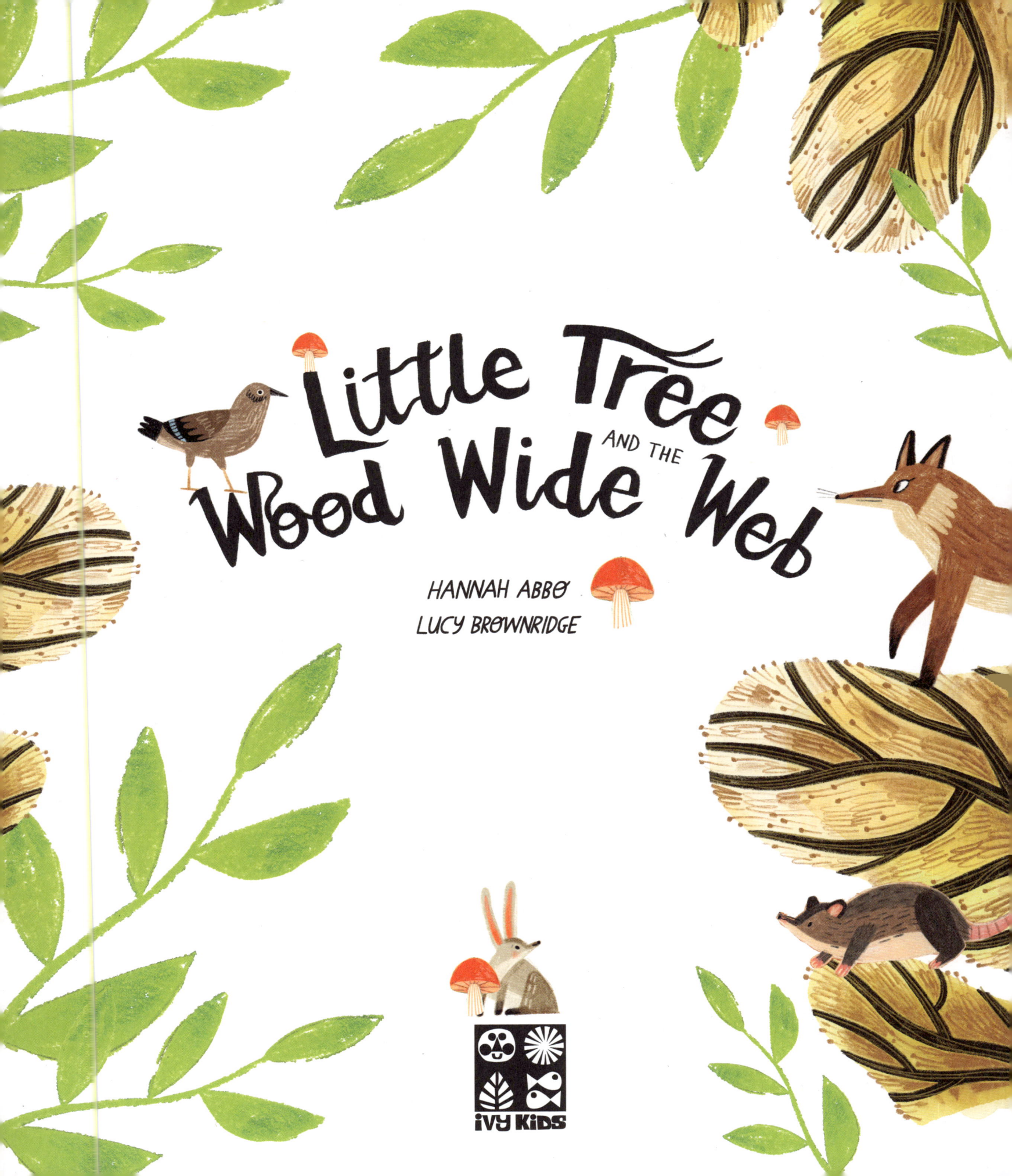

Little Tree and the Wood Wide Web

HANNAH ABBO
LUCY BROWNRIDGE

IVY KIDS

In the ancient forest, a little Douglas fir tree sapling has sprung, and she is excited to grow! Little Tree thought that the world above the ground would be a little bit sunnier. But the big ancient trees are right in the light and keep it very dark on the forest floor.

So, she stretched her branches a little further, unfurled some new green leaves, and toughened the shiny bark around her middle.

Since the first drop of water touched the top of her seed pod and made her grow, there hadn't been any rain in the ancient forest.

When a tree cries, it doesn't just shed regular tears.
Instead, the sadness comes out through its roots and spreads into the earth.

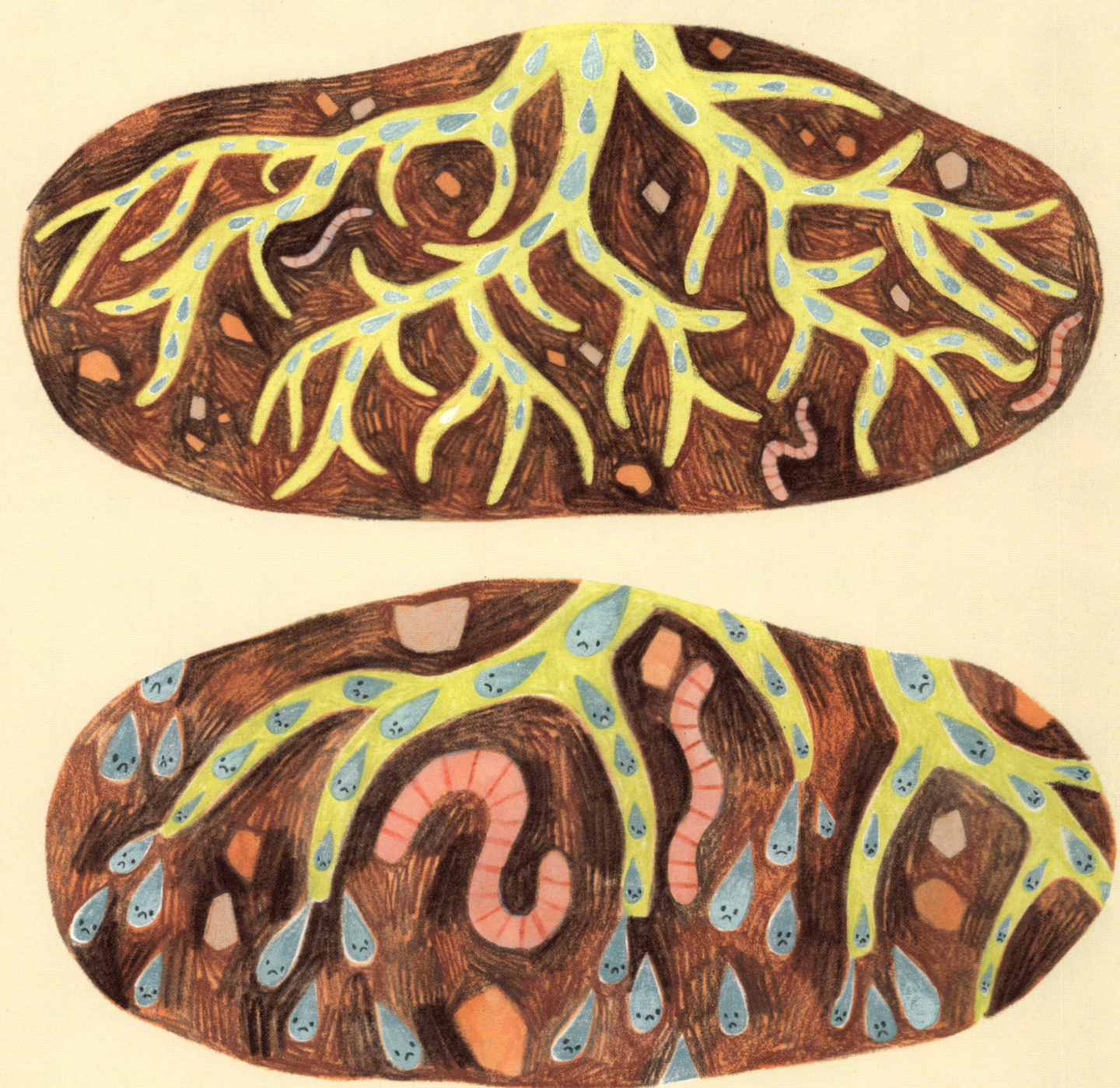

And sure enough, as soon as Little Tree's sadness left her roots,
something extraordinary happened...

"LITTLE TREE NEEDS HELP"

"LITTLE TREE NEEDS HELP"

Her cry traveled from small tree to tall tree, across clearings, and spinneys, and glades, and thickets.
"Little Tree needs help!"
came the message, loud, and clear, and under the ground.

Trees all over the forest, from the very furthest glades and thickets felt the message reach their roots. They sent their replies back through the the Wood Wide Web:

"I'm not very well, I don't have the energy to spare", said one.

"I'm still growing, and I hardly have enough light for myself", came another.

"I'm tired out from growing nuts. They will grow into my babies one day, any water or energy I have spare is for them", replied the last.

The Wood Wide Web had done all it could, but it seemed there was no help to be found in the ancient forest. Perhaps Little Tree was alone after all.

But the message still had one more tree to reach—an elegant paper birch. She wasn't the most magnificent tree in the forest, but she was just tall enough to reach the light perfectly. Her roots passed over an underground stream carrying cool water, so Paper Birch never had to worry about finding a drink.

"I can help Little Tree", thought Paper Birch.

So, she used all her might to send her spare sugar energy and water all the way down to her roots, to be carried away by the Wood Wide Web.

Along the way, a greedy spinney of trees sucked up some of the the spare sugars through their roots! But Paper Birch had been very generous and there was plenty left. There was even plenty of sugar and water for the fungus in the Wood Wide Web to feed itself, too.

By now, Little Tree was wilting with despair. When the sugars and water reached her, she could hardly believe her roots!

So, with Paper Birch's help,
Little Tree grew taller and her trunk became
a little fatter with water over the summer.

She grew new leaves, and even her very first pine cone!
When fall came, the rain arrived, and she didn't need
to use the water from Paper Birch anymore.

You might think Little Tree would have been very happy.

And she was, until night fell and all was still in the ancient forest. Deep down in her trunk, Little Tree felt sad.

"I wish I could find some way to say 'thank you' to Paper Birch".

Winter came, the days grew short and there was very little sunshine. This didn't bother Little Tree—her needle-like leaves could soak up even the smallest chink of sunshine and turn its energy into sugar.

But Paper Birch had lost her leaves in the fall, and she
was struggling to keep herself going with what she had stored.

Usually, she kept a little extra sugar in her trunk, but this year
she had sent all her spares to save Little Tree.
She started to cry, but as you know, when a tree cries
it doesn't shed regular tears.

The not-so-little-any-more Little Tree felt the message reach her roots like a burning fire through the cold earth.
Little Tree sent Paper Birch all the sugars she could spare.
She was an *evergreen tree* and still had all her leaves so she could make enough sugar for both of them.

All through the hard winter, Little Tree sent sugar to Paper Birch, and has done every year since. The two trees are both terribly old now and between them, they have helped many hundreds of trees in the ancient forest.

Lots of the trees in the forest are their children, and grandchildren, and together they all care for each other in different ways for different seasons.

Little Tree is very big now. Even though she's one of the tallest in the ancient forest, she wouldn't say she's the strongest. She knows that the forest is only as strong as its smallest, little tree.

Glossary

Wood Wide Web—A network, made from tiny strands, or hyphae, of fungus. It exists under the forest floor and connects a tree's roots to other trees in the forest. The network enables trees to share all sorts of resources and signals with each other. It can also be called a 'mycorrhizal' or 'hyphal' network.

Sugars—Plants make and use sugars as their main energy source. They need sugars to live, grow, and reproduce.

Paper birch tree—A medium-sized deciduous tree with thin, pale, peeling bark that looks a little like white paper. They can live to up to 150-years-old.

Douglas fir Tree—A very large, evergreen conifer tree in the pine tree family. They can grow to up to 55 metres tall and live for up to a thousand years.

Evergreen tree—A tree that keeps its leaves all-year-round.

Fungus—A type of organism that reproduces using spores. Fungi are often mistaken for plants, but they make up their own separate family. This family includes mushrooms, mould, yeast, and toadstools.

Deciduous tree—A tree that loses its leaves in the fall, and regrows them in the spring.

Conifer—A group of mostly evergreen trees that have needle-like leaves and grow cones.

Canopy—The top layer of a forest. The trees whose branches and leaves reach this layer receive the most sunlight.

Photosynthesis—This is the process plants use to turn sunlight into sugars, which they then use as food. The plant uses energy in the sun's light to change water and a gas called carbon dioxide into sugar and a gas called oxygen.

Symbiotic relationship—A relationship where two or more different species exist together in a way which is good for all of them.

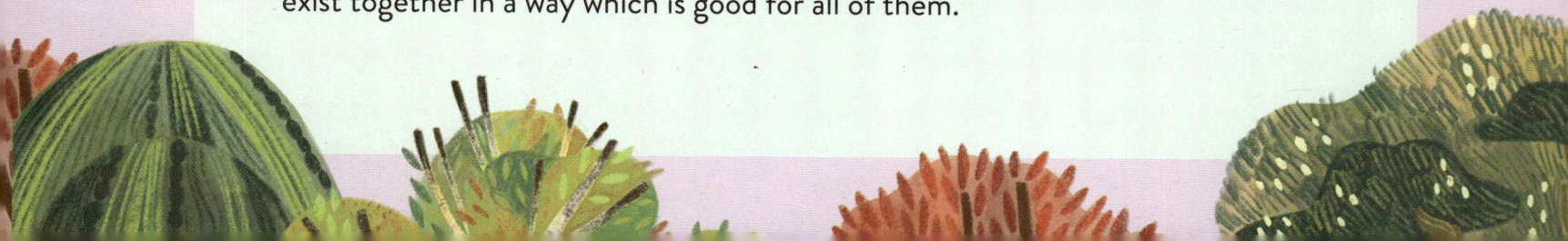

Inspired by the true story

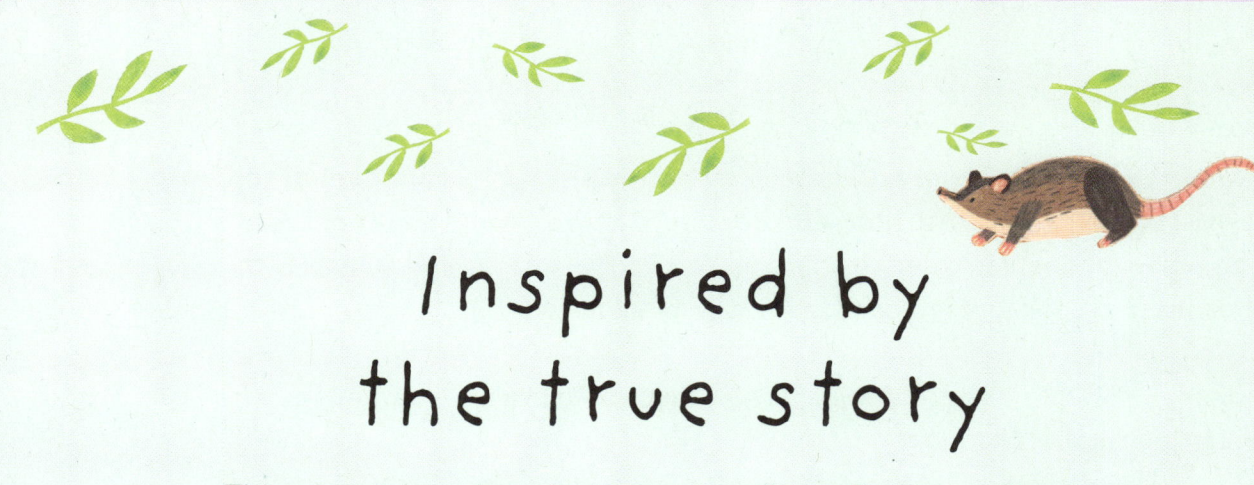

This story is based on the true story of how Professor Suzanne Simard discovered what she came to call 'the Wood Wide Web'. She discovered that through using ancient fungal networks underground, paper birch and Douglas fir trees shared their resources with each other in their times of need. She soon discovered that not only were paper birch and Douglas fir trees connected, but so were all the trees in the forest. They were all part of a thinking, caring, many-species family.

But why does the fungal network do it's job? Because the fungus gets to eat some of the energy it transports around. This sort of relationship in nature, where all benefit, is called a 'symbiotic relationship'.

Even though we have only recently discovered it, the Wood Wide Web isn't new at all. Trees have been using it to help, and talk to each other for millions of years. There is still so much for us to discover, and sometimes the most wonderful things are right beneath our feet.

For Sally, Leo, Emily and Tamara—L.B

Little Tree and the Wood Wide Web © 2023 Quarto Publishing plc.
Text © 2023 Lucy Brownridge.
Illustrations © 2023 Hannah Abbo.

First published in 2023 by Ivy Kids, an imprint of The Quarto Group.
100 Cummings Center, Suite 265D, Beverly, MA 01915 USA.
T +1 978-282-9590 F +1 978-283-2742 www.Quarto.com

The right of Lucy Brownridge to be identified as the author and Hannah Abbo to be identified
as the illustrator of this work has been asserted by them in accordance with the
Copyright, Designs and Patents Act, 1988 (United Kingdom).
All rights reserved.

No part of this publication may be reproduced, stored in a retrieval system, or transmitted,
in any form, or by any means, electrical, mechanical, photocopying, recording, or otherwise without
the prior written permission of the publisher or a license permitting restricted copying.
A catalogue record for this book is available from the British Library.

ISBN 978-0-7112-8487-6
eISBN 978-0-7112-8935-2

The illustrations were created with color pencils
Set in Brandon and Providence

Published by Debbie Foy • Commissioned and edited by Lucy Brownridge •
Designed by Holly Jolley • Production by Dawn Cameron

Manufactured in Europe by Lego S.p.A., LE042023
Printed by a company certified to ISO 14001: 2015 and registered
to the European Union's Eco Management & Audit Scheme.

9 8 7 6 5 4 3 2 1